BLOGGING BASICS

OLA OBEMBE

This book is dedicated to my family and espacially Joshua Ayomide Abba Obembe.

Contents

CHAPTER ONE

The Definition of Blogging

The Definition of Blogging The definition of blogging is something that is very much in flux, as the new technologies that appear every day redefine what a blog is, what a blog can be, and what a blog should do. For many years, blogs were defined as text-based websites that kept records of days, similar to a captain's log on a sailing ship. However, this started to change as the group of people who kept blogs became more diverse.

The more bloggers began to explore the limits of the medium and of the technology that made it possible, the more the boundaries of what could be called a "blog" expanded. Today, photoblogs are abundant, and there are even video blogs as well. Mobile blogging devices may well change the definition of blogging entirely by making it possible for bloggers to create new kinds of posts. Another element of the blogosphere that is starting to redefine blogging is the corporate blog.

As more companies hire writers to keep blogs with the sole purpose of creating positive buzz about their brand, bloggers across the globe are arguing about whether these manufactured blogs are worthy of the name. Between all of these different forces that are constantly expanding and reshaping the blogosphere, it is difficult to imagine that the definition of what is and is not a blog will ever remain fixed for very long.

Niche as the determinant Because there are so many blogs and websites about blogs on the internet, it can be tough to distinguish your blogging website from all of the others. Whether you are starting up a new website aimed at bloggers or whether you are looking to make your existing blogging site more distinctive, the key to building and maintaining a site that will capture the interest and attention of the blogging community is finding your niche. If you can fill a unique need in a way that no other website does, you'll be able to build a lasting readership among web surfers.

Once you have discovered a niche, you will still have a lot to do, but finding your place in the blogosphere is the place to begin. Every great blogging website starts with a great idea, and you can't build a successful site that will last without one. There are many great sites aimed at today's bloggers, and competition for the attention of this growing demographic is fierce. To make your blogging website stand out from the pack, you will need to offer something that no other site is currently offering, or you will need to do the same thing that an already popular site does but in a more impressive or valuable way. One way to discover an ideal model for your blogging website is to look at the sites that have successfully captured a blogging audience already to determine if you can appropriate some of their strategies to help realize your vision.

Of course, you will also need to add a unique flair to your project to stand apart from your competition. Many people agree that the websites that do the best in today's market are the sites that have the most personality. The fiercely individual surfers who are bloggers are a demographic that responds especially strongly to personality, so consider how you can give your site a unique and attractive feeling by lending your voice and sensibility to your site's design and content.

Once you have a great idea for your site, have pinpointed a special niche that you are well equipped to fill, and have infused the site with personality, the next step is figuring out how to get the word out to bloggers. In the long run, a great idea just isn't enough to propel your blogging website to success. You will need to draft a smart and realistic marketing plan to draw readers to your site. Once you hook a blogger, your great content will keep them coming back, but it is vital to get that first glance or your site won't have a chance to shine.

Three Basics For A Great Blog

A blog is a type of online journal that a person can use to post on a variety of different topics. People use Blogs for just about anything including a shared online journal and advertising their business, among others. A lot of people are hesitant to begin a blog because they feel it is complicated, but it is not. Here are three very basic tips to get you started, and before you know it you will be blogging in no time at all. The best thing about blogging is it's free! So follow these steps and start blogging.

1. Content

Think about the content you wish to put into your blog. Is it going to be a personal journal, information on a certain topic, or even a way to advertise your business? No matter what the reason content is important. Start your blog with three of four topics at first. This will begin your blog and get you, visitors, to your site. Most of these visitors will post comments on the topics and when they do, pay attention to them. Look for any questions in these posts; they will probably give you your next topic without even realizing it. Be sure though, before you post your topics you carefully research them. You want to appear as an expert on the subject you are blogging on, so research is extremely important. The more you know about your topic the more of an expert you will appear.

2. Availability

-You need to make yourself available to your visitors. Keep your profile updated and include email instructions for any questions that your visitor may have. The more available you are to the visitor the happier they will be.

3. Personalize

-Once you have your blog created now is the time to add links to affiliates related to your site. One of the most popular sites for bloggers to do this with is Clickbank. There are other sites available besides Clickbank and are fairly easy to find. All you will have to do is go to your search engine and type in advertising affiliates and you will be amazed at the number of returns. Businesses are eager to have their business promoted and are willing to pay people to do this, what a great advantage for a blog. This site will provide you with a lot of different advertisers that you can place on your blog. What is even better is you can make money while advertising. One important thing to remember when you are adding your links is not to go overboard. Too much advertising can turn your visitors away.

No matter what the purpose of your blog maybe if you follow these three easy steps you will be up and blogging in no time. What is even better is when you add the affiliate links you can make great money too without even trying.

CHAPTER TWO

Blogging 101

Blogging 101 is mostly about the blogging vocabulary. To understand blogs, you need to know the terms blog, platform, domain, and web host. Once you have mastered these key elements of blogging, you can enter any conversation about blogging with confidence. After you know what exactly a blog is, you will be on your way to passing the final exam of blogging 101. A blog is short for weblog, which simply means a series of online posts presented in reverse chronological order.

That's all! Most blogs are text, but there are also photo blogs and video blogs. The rest of blogging 101 has to do with the technical side of things. If you are setting up a blog, you will need a platform, a web host, and a domain. A blogging platform is a computer software program that allows you to write posts and update your blog. Your platform is also what you use to design the look of your blog, from color scheme to font size. The web host is sort of like the virtual file cabinet where your blog is stored. Your computer communicates with the host when you upload or edit a post. The domain is the online address of your blog and usually ends in 'dot com'. Now that you know what a blog is, what a platform is, and what domains and hosts are, congratulate yourself! You have passed blogging 101. Blogging: Consolidation, Debt, and New Information Technology If you are interested in blogging, consolidation, debt, and other financial topics are sure to appear in many of the blogs that you regularly read.

Techniques to make and manage money are some of the most popular topics for bloggers to explore on the web, so it is little wonder that so many bloggers turn their attention to dealing with debt. Falling into debt is all too easy, and getting out of debt can be very difficult for people who do not have a lot of financial expertise. For people who have a knack for dealing with finances, blogging about their insights and knowledge can be a great way to literally and figuratively share the wealth. If you are considering getting into blogging, consolidation, debt, savings, and investment topics can prove to be very fruitful things to write about.

Many professional bloggers who make a living off of their blogs spend their days writing about money. If you know how to court advertisers and build a blog fan base, you can make money just by talking about money. If you are familiar with loan consolidation, negotiating settlements with credit card companies, or any other financial topics, consider using your knowledge to create a successful blog.

By sharing your expertise, you may be able to help your readers get out of debt while you reap sizable monetary rewards for your time and knowledge. If You are Already Blogging, Money May be Just a Click Away If you already spend a fair amount of time blogging, money may come to you as soon as you ask for it. Once you have an established blog with a regular readership, it is easy to turn a profit through advertising. By hosting sponsored links or banners, you can see income from your hobby almost overnight. Even if you did not start your blog intending to turn a profit, making supplementary income from your blog may be easier than you think. Of course, even for people who have spent months or years blogging, money from advertising revenue may not add up to a large sum.

The amount of money that you can make as a blogger depends on a lot of different factors, but perhaps the most important element of the equation is the topic of your blog. If your blog is on a subject that appeals to a demographic that advertisers have a strong desire to reach, you will be more likely to be able to turn a large profit on your blog than if your blog is on a fairly obscure subject that does not draw the kind of audience that advertisers need to appeal to. Of course, the only way to find out where you fall on this spectrum is to try hosting some ads. If you are already blogging, you have nothing to lose.

Blog Ethics

Creating a blog is a great way for anyone to share their life experiences and even advertise their business. To date, there is no actual code of ethics developed for bloggers to follow but there are three common-sense ethic codes that anyone should follow while they are running their blog posts. These are the code of ethics that will prove you as a trustworthy blog owner.

1. Fair and Honest:

You need to be fair and honest to your followers. You need to make sure all the information you provide is honest without adding any false information. When you are providing facts you need to make them distinct, true, and easy to follow. Do not attempt to distort your facts, visitors can read this right away and as a result, you will lose visitors. If you happen to provide any information, on your site that may appear to be false; you need to provide your reader with factual information to back up your statement. If you are adding pictures to your blog add captions underneath to explain to the reader about the picture. Fair and Honest are two of the most important components of the blogger's code of ethics.

2. Harm of others:

When you are creating a blog topic on a very controversial issue avoid using any ones names or places. This will protect you from any lawsuits and also from hurting visitors' feelings. A good motto for this code of ethics would be, to say to others what you would want them to say about you. You also need to be sure that you protect a person's privacy. Invading a person's privacy is rude as well as intrusive. If you do not want someone doing it to you then do not do it to others. A great way to avoid violating this blog code of ethics is to avoid using names or places if it is all possible. If it is unavoidable try to use as much damage control as possible.

3. Be Accountable:

You need to accept the consequences that may come with your blog. If you have made a mistake in any of your postings admit it right away, do not try to avoid it. Everyone makes mistakes and if you own up to yours you will be more respected in the reader's eyes.

If someone happens to question your information on your blog open up a discussion with the person. Try to see why they feel the way they do and if they prove to be right, apologize to the person and admit that yes you are right I did make a mistake. If you are not accountable for your blog you will violate the blog code of ethics and as a result, you will lose followers.

All of these blog codes of ethics are common sense but also the most neglected parts of Blogging. Following a basic code of ethics will enable you to be a trustworthy blogger to your visitors.

CHAPTER THREE

Personal Blogging, Documentary, and History

When it comes to personal blogging, the documentary is the default genre. There are plenty of blogs that serve other functions, but many blogs are primarily catalogs of the life experiences of their author. Although there are quite a few blogs that focus on collecting poetry and other forms of creative writing, the vast majority of personal blogs are in some sense documentaries. For many years, the act of making a documentary was meant to be an objective act of reporting the sights and sounds that the filmmaker, writer, or photographer encountered. However, in contemporary times there has been a movement towards embracing the subjectivity inherent in the documentary form.

This means that modern documentaries often reflect the distinctive voice and sensibility of their creator, and the fact that today's documentaries often revolve around personality blurs the lines between documentary and memoir. Blogs rest somewhere between these two genres, muddying the distinctions even further. Personal blogging, documentary, and memoir are now irrevocably intertwined, for better or for worse. Although few bloggers think of themselves as making documentaries in any formal sense, every time somebody sits down in front of a computer and types up a record of their day, they are documenting their historical moment. The things that we take for granted about our daily lives, like the way that we use specific modes of transportation, or the kinds of products that we buy, often seem quite fascinating to people who live in circumstances different from ours, and it is this kind of fascination that is at the heart of many documentary projects.

When people think about blogging, the documentary is not very likely to be the first adjective that crosses their minds, but a few decades down the road it is very likely that today's blogs will be seen primarily as very subjective documentaries of our era. The people of tomorrow will almost certainly look to the blogs of today for insight into our historical moment. When it comes to blogging, the documentary may not be the aim of most people who spend their time posting their thoughts and ideas on the internet. In some ways, the documentary aspect of blogging is more of a side effect than a primary goal. However, the fact that so many people are interested in publishing these public online diaries shows that personal blogs are about more than just rumination. The fact that bloggers are so stimulated by and interested in sharing their ideas reinforces the idea that personal blogs are, in some ways, documentaries meant for public consumption. Documentaries appeal to people who are curious about other ways of life, and many people who regularly read others' blogs are looking for this same kind of new perspective.

Blogging Teens Every day, blogs are created by people of all ages and from all walks of life, but when it comes to blogging, teen writers are truly on the cutting edge of the movement. Because today's teenagers are the first generation of people to have grown up using the internet at every stage of their development, many adolescents have a seemingly innate sense of how to use web technology to express their innermost thoughts and ideas. Older writers often experience a kind of learning curve when they begin to blog, but many young people find that using a word processor and blogging software feels more natural and direct a mode of communication than writing in a diary ever could. One of the reasons why blogs have undergone a kind of explosion in the teen community and are growing by leaps and bounds is the fact that they provide a unique mixture of visibility and anonymity. A teenager can invite friends and peers to read his or her blog with a simple email, thereby winning attention or possibly even praise. Of course, with visibility usually comes the possibility of embarrassment, but the fact that it is possible to blog anonymously with an invented handle or nickname negates a lot of the potential for humiliation.

Many a blogging teen lives in fear that a parent or guardian will discover his or her blog, but by publishing under an alias a teenager can spill his or her secrets without fear of being traced. Outside the world of blogging, teen writers often have very limited opportunities to be published. Magazines and journals are often reticent to publish young writers who may not have as much credibility as older writers with a lot of experience and extensive credits to their names. This can discourage adolescents from writing or from seeking chances to publish their work. By blogging, young people can begin to gain a following of readers without first having to win the attention and support of an editor or publisher who may not be very interested in teenage authors. Between the fact that blogs provide young people with a chance to exercise their impressive technical aptitude, to gain visibility without compromising privacy, and to build a readership for their writing without having to jump through the traditional hoops of the publishing industry, it is little wonder that are so many teenagers with blogs. For some teenagers, blogging is even a very social endeavor that allows them to meet people with similar interests from all over the world.

Many a blogging teen has discovered that having a weblog on the internet is a great way to explore self-expression and, often, to win positive feedback from new friends. Choosing The Right Free Blogging Tools There are many free blogging tools on the market, but loading up your blog with all of the free accessories that you can find isn't necessarily a good idea. While it may be tempting to add a visitor counter, a flashy background, an exciting new font, and a cluster of quirky animated gifs to your blog, this kind of plan can easily backfire. The key to getting the most from free blog tools is being selective. It is a great idea to learn about all of the kinds of free blogging tools that are available so that you can make an informed decision about what to add to your blog, but try to remember that just because you can have something doesn't mean that you need it. Practice restraint and only choose the options that you think will be useful. If you can find out how many visitors are reading your blog by checking your traffic statistics, a visitor counter is likely to add unnecessary clutter to your page. If your blog is text-based, a flashy background can be more of a distraction than a benefit. Be realistic about assessing what kinds of blog accessories will help you realize your vision and improve your site. Remember that even a blog tool that doesn't cost you any cash may not be an asset in the long run.

Popularity Of Blogs

Blogs have become very popular in recent years. They are great ways for a person to share their ideas and thoughts in a public forum. They come from all over the world and each one is jam-packed with different cultures, beliefs, and thoughts. They are also great for creating an online community that happens to have the same idea or beliefs. Some bloggers are even making money with their blogs. There are so many reasons why they have become popular the list is endless.

1. Easy to use

Blogs are easy to create because they have support from many different standard technologies. You can create a blog with little or no hassle and most of them provide you with a free template that you can use to create your blog. You can also use the information on other blogs to help in creating your own. You as a reader are also able to post comments on a blog without any problems. All of these combined add to the popularity of blogs. No one ones to go through a hassle to get their thoughts and ideas published on the internet

2. Easy to set up

There are many different types of software that are available that can assist you in setting up your blog. You do not need to be a computer geek to learn how to create them, nor do you need a degree in computers. It has been said that blogs are so easy to create a kid can do it. There is also software available that will assist you in keeping your blog organized when you have finished setting it up.

3. Human

As anyone who knows who works, or even thinks, about computers knows that every site out there has been created by a human being. Well, the same is true with blogs. Behind every screen, there is a human person just like you. What makes the blogs so popular is behind every human lies many different cultures and beliefs. Blogging is a great way to bring these different cultures together in one place.

4. Search Engines

Search engines love blogs because they are usually jam-packed with keywords. Another reason why search engines love blogs is that they are updated regularly and search engines love up-to-date information.

5. Versatile

Blogs are very versatile. They are easy to place comments, calendars, and announcements among others. They are a great way to communicate important points as well.

These are just a few of the reasons why blogs have become so popular in recent years. Blogs are a very important part of almost anyone's life. If you ask someone you know it's a high chance they will tell you that they have a blog site.

CHAPTER FOUR

How to Learn new Blogging Softwares

A lot of blogging software is specifically designed to be simple to use, but even the least intimidating blogging program can feel very overwhelming to somebody who has not spent a lot of time learning the ins and outs of different kinds of software. Particularly for newer bloggers, learning how to use the interface of blogging software is the most difficult part of blogging. If you are somebody who feels comfortable expressing themselves in another medium, it may prove to be well worth your time and effort to learn blogging software, but that doesn't mean that the task will be easy.

The main thing that will help you find success as you learn how to use a new kind of blogging software is to try and take things slowly. Many people get so excited about learning to blog that they try to rush into the thick of it and start exploring the most complicated features of a program right away. This can lead to getting confused and feeling frustrated, and all too many potential bloggers burn out during this stage of the process. If you take your time learning the basics of your blog software program before you move on to more advanced techniques, you will be more likely to retain what you have learned, and to keep feeling positive about your ability to understand the world of blogging. Mobile Blogging is on the Cutting Edge Mobile blogging is an exciting phenomenon that is sweeping the blogosphere.

One of the reasons why a lot of bloggers are attracted to the medium of blogging in the first place is that they enjoy being able to make frequent updates and posts that keep all of their visitors up to speed with current situations. Mobile blogs, or "moblogs," take this to the extreme by allowing users to post things literally as they happen. This new wave of moblogs and mobloggers keeps web surfers up to date with good and bad events of importance as they occur all over the world, helping to make international communication faster and more accurate. Many people feel that the limitations of blogging have a lot to do with geography. After all, there is only so current that a blog can be when you need to run home and boot up to update it.

However, mobile blogging marks the beginning of a thrilling new era when web-based communication can happen spontaneously from any location. Moblogging devices mean that there is almost nowhere on the planet that remains off-limits for bloggers. Mobile blogging is still in its infancy because the technology that makes it possible has only recently hit the global market. The first moblog technology became available over a decade ago, but it is only in the past two or three years that mobile web devices have become user-friendly enough to appeal to most consumers.

As camera phones and other mobile technology become more popular, more and more bloggers are getting away from their desks and are hitting the streets. Moblogging is becoming much more widespread than it was even a few months ago, and mobloggers are quickly attracting a lot of attention from the blogging community. It is not yet clear whether moblogs will become the dominant kinds of blogs in the years to come, but the current trend seems to imply that moblogs are here to stay. Mobile devices make it possible to blog from the sites where current events are unfolding, which is one of the reasons why mobile blogging has so much thrilling potential to revolutionize the blogosphere.

A moblogger with a camera phone can post blog entries from, say, the foot of the podium at a presidential speech, or from the stands during the final moments of the world series. This enables bloggers to experience the same real-time thrills that live television coverage provides, but in a more democratic medium. The combination of mobility and individual control that moblogging provides certainly places mobloggers on the cutting edge of today's communications technology, and it is hard to imagine that the number and prestige of moblogs will not continue to grow in the coming years.

CHAPTER FIVE

Your New Baby, Blogging, and Modern Motherhood

For the mother of a new baby, blogging is likely to be the last thing on her mind. Taking care of an infant is an almost incredible amount of work, and between changing diapers and putting the final touches on the nursery, it seems unrealistic to imagine that there would be time left over for any mother to blog. However, a growing number of new moms are joining the blogosphere to share their experiences during this exciting time of life. There is a whole range of benefits that new mothers can reap from blogging, and the spectrum covers everything from getting through the night to helping distant relatives feel closer.

Among the reasons why, for a mom dealing with the hassles and triumphs of a baby, blogging is a great idea, is that having a blog about motherhood is a great way to blow off some steam. Babies often have very erratic sleep patterns that leave parents up at odd hours of the night, and sometimes the best way to fill those hours is on the internet. Many new moms turn to television to help them weather these dawn vigils, but by blogging through the night moms can turn what feels like a somewhat depressing situation into an actively positive and productive one. Another reason why new moms often find blogging very satisfying is that it helps them to be a part of a community. For moms who are not able to successfully juggle a full social life with the very tough demands of taking care of a new baby, blogging can be a great way to stave off the isolation that sometimes comes with this stage of life.

A baby requires constant attention, and it can be difficult to attend social gatherings or events when you are responsible for an infant. Luckily, the blogosphere is full of other moms in the same situation, and by chatting with them it is possible to overcome some of the loneliness that many new mothers are surprised to encounter. Of course, for a mom with an adorable new baby, blogging can be as much about celebration as it is about necessity. Having a blog about living with a new child can give mothers the chance to reflect on how powerful and warm the sensation of motherhood is, and sometimes sharing the triumphs of this unique time can make them even sweeter. A blog is a great way to keep friends and family updated with news about your baby's first words or first steps, and with new technology, it is easier than ever to take photos and video clips a part of your blog, so you can give far-away relatives the chance to feel much more involved in your child's life.

CHAPTER SIX

Photo Blogging as the Pinnacle of Modern Technology

Many people feel that photo blogging is the most exciting kind of blogging that exists. Building and maintaining a photoblog is no more difficult than creating and updating a text-based blog, and many people feel that the internet's high-speed, full-color technology reaches the pinnacle of its appeal with the transmission of images. Posting photographs in a blog format on a daily, weekly, or occasional basis is a great way to express yourself while reaching viewers in an emotionally charged and aesthetically engaging way, and surfing photo blogs can help you to get a whole new perspective on the world in which we live.

Many people who run image blogs are photographers by trade, but photo blogging is also very popular among hobbyists and amateur shutterbugs. To be certain, a lot of the most popular photoblogs have gained attention because the pictures on them are of the highest artistic caliber, and a lot of the people who run these striking blogs are graduates of prestigious art schools and have impressive professional portfolios. However, some of the most well-known and most often visited photo blogs are as notable for their concepts as for the pictures themselves. Certain photo blogs, like the popular "Cute Overload" which features picture after picture of adorable animals, are more about the thematic content of the pictures than they are about the style in which the snapshots are taken.

The fact that photo blogs range from forums to display the work of highly skilled artisans to playful collections of curiosities shows that photo blogging is a truly diverse form. The fact that photo blogs are so easy to build and to update makes this kind of visual communication very democratic and enables people at all skill levels to become a part of the global conversation about the nature and value of photography today. Whether you are an artist or hobbyist who wants to create a photoblog, or whether you are just somebody who enjoys learning about new places and things, spending some time looking at the most popular photography blogs on the internet can be a very rewarding endeavor.

You can travel to another place or another time by seeing pictures of faraway locations and long-gone eras. You can see your neighborhood with fresh eyes by discovering how local artists have photographed the town or city in which you live. Photo blogging allows people to communicate all of these things and more, which makes it a very exciting part of the modern blogosphere. If the best thing about web technology is that it allows people to reach each other in a very personal way from across great distances, then in many ways photo blogs are the most successful kind of web sites.

The Pros and Cons of Video Blogging Video blogging have a lot of advantages over text-based blogging, and it is little wonder that this new technology is catching on all over the globe. Video blogs very effectively grab the attention of web surfers, and people are much more likely to become excited about the dynamic content of a video blog than they are likely to find a written posting very thrilling. The more enthusiastic viewers are about a site, the quicker the word of mouth spreads, and the more traffic the site will get. Of course, there are plenty of disadvantages to video blogging as well. Hosting a v-blog requires quite a bit of server space, which can make it difficult to get started. It takes more time to process and upload a video file than it does to dash off a quick bit of text, which means that running and updating a video blog can be quite a bit of work. In addition, web surfers sometimes grow frustrated with the slow loading times of the files on many video blogs. Whether you opt for a video blog or not depends on what kind of subject matter you want to cover, and how much time you can devote to video blogging. Before you decide to pursue a video blog, consider if there is an easier way for you to get your message across.

CHAPTER SEVEN

What Is a Blogging Community?

The term Blogging Community stands as an inspiring example of a successful online community where the ever-increasing numbers of affiliated members enjoy a fertile environment for discussion and debate about the ideas that shape the face of their Country or business. A good example is one of the many authors affiliated with the conservative Canadian community known as The Blogging Tories. Today, there are over a hundred and fifty text-based blogs Communities with the group, and there are new Bloggers every day.

The majority of Community bloggers do make political events and topics the focus of their blogs, but not all of the content that a Blogging Community creates and publishes is overtly related to the movements of the Canadian parliament or the prime minister. Although the community members were brought together by a shared conservative viewpoint, the fact that not all of the postings on all of the member's blogs focus on political topics is one of the most exciting things about the Blogging Tories.

On any given day, the main website's blogroll may feature postings about Olympic medalists, a James Bond film festival in Quebec, or a comical personal experience with a telemarketer. The idea that having a political affiliation in common makes it possible to have a fruitful discussion about other kinds of topics has interesting implications for how online communities are established and how they grow. The Exciting New Frontier Of Professional Blogging Professional blogging is a very new idea with a lot of potential for entrepreneurs who have insight, drive, and a basic understanding of today's innovative web technology.

The ranks of so-called pro bloggers are still quite small, and there are very few people who make their living entirely off of their blogs. However, every day there are more and more people who have managed to turn their weblogs into cash cows that supplement their income. The number of pro bloggers is growing by leaps and bounds, but it is difficult to say whether this trend will continue. Many bloggers dream of entering the sphere of professional blogging. There are very few people who happily devote an hour or more each day to their blog without at least occasionally wishing that they could earn some kind of financial reward for all of their work.

Several models exist for making money with a blog, the most popular being to sell advertising space through Google's AdSense program or directly to a company that wishes to reach the demographic that your blog appeals to. However, there are very few people indeed who can make a comfortable living just by selling space on their blog sidebars. A lot of the people who read weblogs are bloggers themselves, in part because the people who use blogging technology daily are most likely to be interested in what other writers are doing with the medium.

This fact begins to explain why the people who succeed in the world of professional blogging are mostly people who have devoted themselves almost entirely to learning about, talking about, and writing about blogging. More than any other topic, pro bloggers turn their attention to the phenomenon of blogging itself. A lot of pro bloggers make the topic of blogging the stunningly self-reflexive ongoing focus of their blogs. Of course, professional blogging is destined to become much more complicated in the future than it is today. In the current moment, pro bloggers who attract the largest audiences and make the most money are mostly concerned with investigating the blogging movement and with offering advice to amateur bloggers. However, as the kinds of people who regularly read blogs change, and the demographics of bloggers expand and diversify as blogging software becomes more user-friendly, it is very likely indeed that the world of pro blogging will begin to reflect these changes. Indeed, it is very difficult to predict exactly what kinds of blogs will be reaping the greatest financial rewards five or ten years down the road. The world of pro blogging is one of constant change and flux, which is part of what makes it so exciting.

9 798886 294842

Printed by Libri Plureos GmbH in Hamburg,
Germany